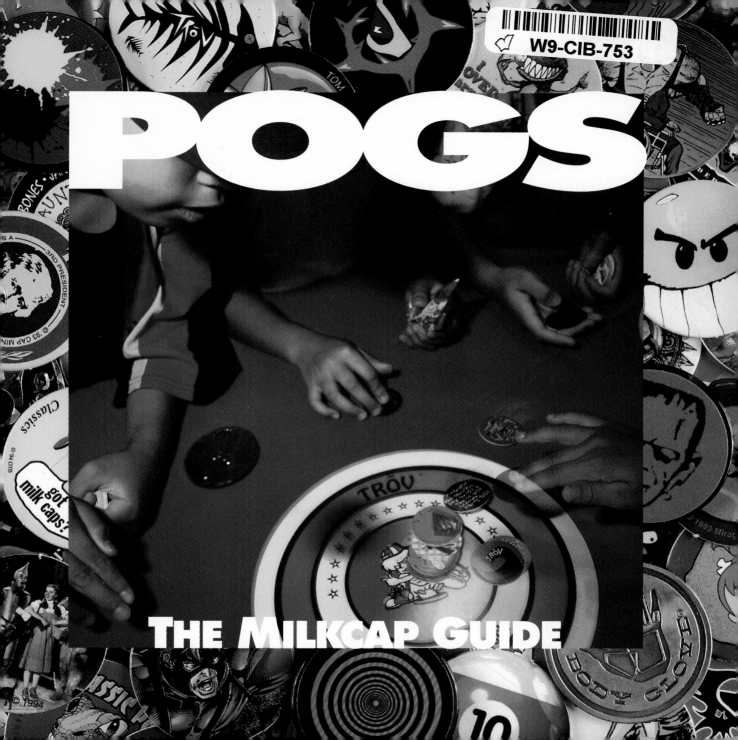

POGS

THE MILKCAP GUIDE

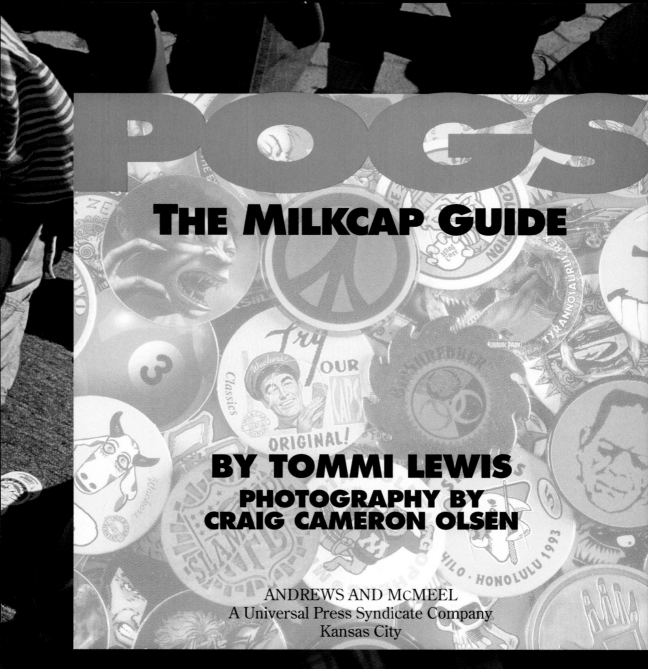

POGS

THE MILKCAP GUIDE

BY TOMMI LEWIS
PHOTOGRAPHY BY CRAIG CAMERON OLSEN

ANDREWS AND MCMEEL
A Universal Press Syndicate Company
Kansas City

ISBN: 0-8362-4240-8

First printing, November 1994
Third printing, July 1995

Written By: Tommi Lewis
Photography By: Craig Cameron Olsen
Book Design By: Steven Stewart
Additional Reporting By: Kim Lockhart

ACKNOWLEDGMENTS
Thanks for editing support from Karen Good. Thanks also to Melanie Ching and all
the milkcap manufacturers who were interviewed and contributed samples for
photographs; Tom Thornton and Jean Lowe at Andrews and McMeel who made
writing this book fun; my colleagues at DISNEY ADVENTURES . . . I'll miss you guys!
And most especially to Peter and my family— my heart and soul. Special thanks to
my 12-year-old stepson, Benjamin, who is forever cool.

contents

CHAPTER 1

A pog is a trov is a jot is a...

MILKCAP! Makes no difference. Whatever you call them, they are pretty much the same glossy, cardboard caps kids love to play, collect and trade. And kids all over are going **POG WILD!** ● The name **POG** comes from Passion Orange Guava, a juice produced by a dairy in Hawaii. To help promote the juice, the dairy printed the letters **"POG"** on the caps of its old-fashioned milk bottles. Local kids collected and played with the milkcaps, and soon began calling the milkcap game **"POG."** ● This book will give you valuable tips on how to collect **POGs** (also called milkcaps or caps for short), different ways to play the milkcap game, plus information on tournaments, promotional caps, manufacturers and much more! ● Before diving into the rest of this jam-packed milkcap guide, check out this chapter's color photos of some of the best looking caps around.

PACIFIC RIM™   Wicked Witch of the West   © 1994 TEC

JOTS™   Fireball   4

PACIFIC RIM™   Black and White series

TROV™   Zebra

SPONTANEOUS ENTERPRISES   WHISKERS   Whiskers   3

SPONTANEOUS ENTERPRISES

BIG APPLE COLLECTORS   RUDE BOY   HZZ HZZ HZZ

WORLD POG™ FEDERATION   I LOVED BARNEY™   Junk Food III

7

SLAM CO™   Super Mario Bros.   MORTON

AMERICAN GAME CAPS™   GALAXY ROYALTY   Prince Buzz Armstrong   Galaxy Royalty series

TK CAPS

TK CAPS   X RAY SPECS

Modern day milkcap

Dolly Madison   QUALITY CHEKD   GRADE A   PASTEURIZED   HOMOGENIZED MILK   VITAMIN D

caps

hot cap gallery

TK KAPS

TK KAPS

PACIFIC RIM™ Quiksilver

PACIFIC RIM™ Quiksilver

WORLD POG™ FEDERATION Limited 1 of 50,000

PACIFIC RIM™ Tom and Jerry

PACIFIC RIM™ Tom and Jerry

TK CAPS

8

TK KAPS

TROV™

SPONTANEOUS ENTERPRISES

SPONTANEOUS ENTERPRISES Cap Flingers

Pound'n Gorilla

Z COMIC CAPS

JAM CAPS

PACIFIC RIM™ King Kong

PACIFIC RIM™ Black and White series

TK KAPS

PACIFIC RIM™

WACKERS™ — Windshield Wackers' Splatter Bug

WACKERS™ — Windshield Wackers' Splatter Bug

JAM CAPS — Soccer Series

SLAM CO™ — Marvel's Spider Man

PACIFIC RIM™ — Vancouver Voodoo Roller Hockey

WORLD POG™ FEDERATION

JAM CAPS

SPONTANEOUS ENTERPRISES — Yin and Yang

PACIFIC RIM™ — Eye Series

PACIFIC RIM™ — Quiksilver

SPONTANEOUS ENTERPRISES — Dead End

TK KAPS

TK KAPS

JAM CAPS

9

COLLEGIATE CAPS™   Crimson Tide

CRIMSON TIDE

MLM '94

SPONTANEOUS ENTERPRISES   Shida

SHIDA

©1994 S.G.I.

AMERICAN GAME CAPS™

AGC™

TROV™

TK KAPS

CARD CAPS BY CUSTOM CAPS™   Robert E. Lee

BATTLE OF GAINES'S MILL
27-28 June 1862

ROBERT E. LEE U.S.A.

CUSTOM CAPS™   Carcharadon Carcharias

GREAT WHITE SHARK

Carcharodon carcharias

BUENA VISTA HOME VIDEO   Snow White series

DOPEY

10

TK KAPS

TROV™

U. S. a.

SLAM CO™   Teenage Mutant Ninja Turtles

SlamCo 1.5 © 1993 Mirage Studios

UPPER DECK   Wild K.A.P.S.

SPONTANEOUS ENTERPRISES

FRUITY CAPS

S.E.I.©'94

SPONTANEOUS ENTERPRISES

FRUITY CAPS

S.E.I.©'94

WORLD POG™ FEDERATION   Chagrinned

COLLECT-A-CAP   Power Caps series

Jason

PACIFIC RIM™ — RED CLOUD

PACIFIC RIM™ — Eye Series

SPONTANEOUS ENTERPRISES™ — Cool Helmet

SPONTANEOUS ENTERPRISES™ — Fragile - Handle With Care

BIG APPLE COLLECTORS — PONG STINK

PACIFIC RIM™ — Flintstones

TK KAPS

WACKERS™ — JANGLEBONES BIXBY — Bixby

WORLD POG FEDERATION™ — THE GREAT ONE — Wayne Gretzky "Most Goals"

UNIVERSAL POGS™ — City of Huntington Beach Limited Edition

CARD CAPS BY CUSTOM CAPS™ — ONE HUNDRED DOLLARS — U.S. Currency Set

PACIFIC RIM™ — Tin Man

AMERICAN GAME CAPS™ — MAKES NO SENSE — Poison Circle

AMERICAN GAME CAPS™ — IMMUNE TO POISON

AMERICAN GAME CAPS™ — Poison Everywhere!

AMERICAN GAME CAPS™ — POISON KAP KING — Poison Kap King

11

JOTS™ Spitbull

JOTS™ Spike

TK CAPS

PACIFIC RIM™ Three Twins

SKYCAPS™ Jim Lee

PACIFIC RIM™ Eye Series

SPI KAPS™ Halloween Pumpkin

SKYCAPS™ Superman

SPI KAPS™

PACIFIC RIM™ Warp

JAM CAPS™

JOTS™ Fireball

PACIFIC RIM™ No Fear

WORLD POG™ FEDERATION

JAM CAPS

PACIFIC RIM™ Eye Series

12

TK KAPS Frankenstein

WORLD POG FEDERATION™ Knott's Berry Farm Mystery Lodge

AMERICAN GAME CAPS™ Poison Pirate

TK KAPS Ink Spots

SPI KAP OFFICIAL SPI-KAP

UNIVERSAL POGS™ Legend of Sports

TROV™ Trouncer

LASERFORM™ NFL Lasercap (wooden)

SPONTANEOUS ENTERPRISES

SPONTANEOUS ENTERPRISES

JOTS™ Magnum Slammer

TK KAPS

WORLD POG™ FEDERATION

CAL CAPS Bonehead

TROV™ OctaTROV™

TROV™ OctaTROV™

13

slammer heaven

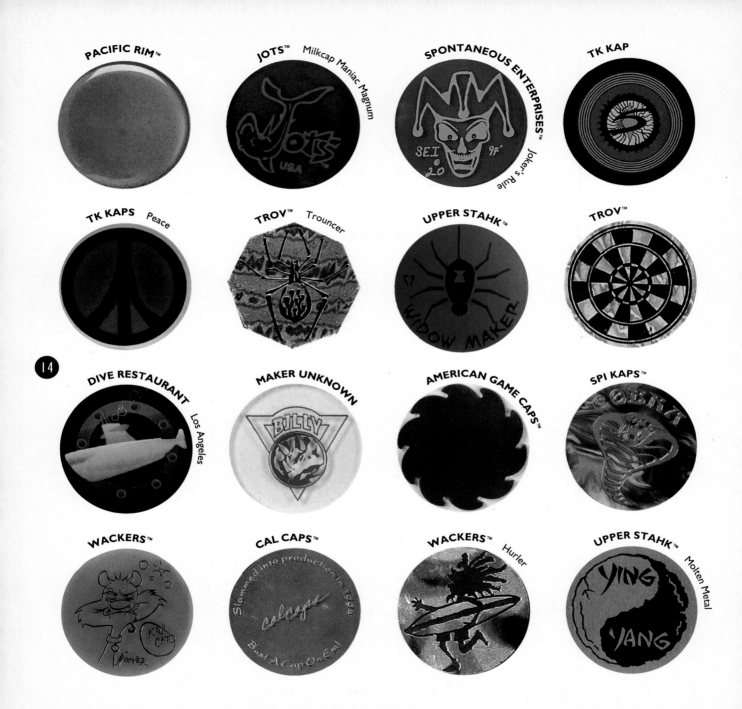

PACIFIC RIM™

JOTS™ Milkcap Maniac Magnum

SPONTANEOUS ENTERPRISES™ Joker's Rule

TK KAP

TK KAPS Peace

TROV™ Trouncer

UPPER STAHK™

TROV™

DIVE RESTAURANT Los Angeles

MAKER UNKNOWN

AMERICAN GAME CAPS™

SPI KAPS™

WACKERS™

CAL CAPS™

WACKERS™ Hurler

UPPER STAHK™ Molten Metal

14

cap holders 'n' more

UPPER STAHK™ Rohk Blasterdome

Mini cap holders by **JOTS**™

TROV™ Coffins

TROV™ Trouncin' Pad

UPPER STAHK™ Lava Tubes

There is more than one way to play, store...

15

"Milkcap Eggcrate Briefcase" by **SPONTANEOUS ENTERPRISES**

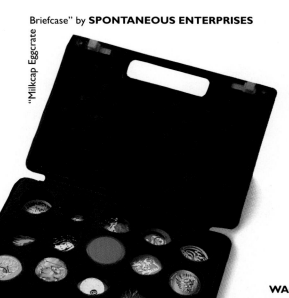

UPPER STAHK™

Rohk Blasterdome

WACKERS™ Game Board

Mini cap holders by **PACIFIC RIM**™

UPPER STAHK™ Nomad

UPPER STAHK™ Warrior Kine

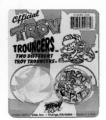

individually or in sheets and sets like these

Caps foil sets

Caps can be purchased

Caps (for your head) by **JOTS**™ and **TROV**™

...and score milkcaps!

JOTS™ Fireball set

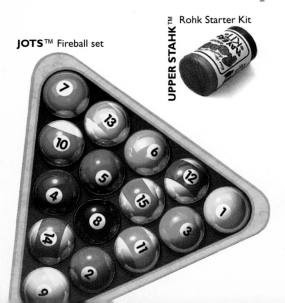

UPPER STAHK™ Rohk Starter Kit

AMERICAN GAME CAPS™ Poison Pirate

AMERICAN GAME CAPS™ Original Milkcap Board

AMERICAN GAME CAPS™ Poison Tube

16

sport pogs

PACIFIC RIM™ Roller Hockey

PACIFIC RIM™ Roller Hockey

COLLEGIATE CAPS™

COLLEGIATE CAPS™

PACIFIC RIM™ Roller Hockey

COLLEGIATE CAPS™

PACIFIC RIM™ Roller Hockey

JAM CAPS

COLLEGIATE CAPS™

COLLEGIATE CAPS™

COLLEGIATE CAPS™

LASERFORM™

COLLEGIATE CAPS™

LASERFORM™

LASERFORM™

LASERFORM™

17

message pogs

VAN NUYS DIVISION LAPD

PACIFIC RIM™

WACKER™

AMERICAN GAME CAPS™

TK KAPS

SPONTANEOUS ENTERPRISES

WACKER™

BONDITERBOPPERS™

WACKER™

SPONTANEOUS ENTERPRISES

SPONTANEOUS ENTERPRISES

UPPER STAHK™

PACIFIC RIM™

SPONTANEOUS ENTERPRISES

TK KAPS

TK KAPS

18

the milk

cap story

From Menkos

bottles

Some cap experts think modern-day milkcap games may have come from a 600-year-old Japanese game called "menkos." Menkos (which means "small mask" in Japanese) were made of clay, ceramic or wood, and were the same size as modern day milkcaps. They sported brightly colored images of sumo wrestlers, samurai warriors and other Japanese icons. In Japan, children stacked and flipped them in the same way the game is played today.

Around the turn of the century, Japanese settlers came to Hawaii, bringing their food, customs, games—and most likely, menkos. Melanie Ching, author of *The Bottlecap Map,* remembers menkos as rectangular cardboard pieces. She said menkos were thicker than today's milkcaps and it took a hard slap with another menko to flip one over.

From the early 1900s until the 1960s, milk in Hawaii came in bottles. Kids discovered

to Milkcaps?

that the milk bottle's waxed cardboard caps had a springiness to them—perfect for stacking and slamming! So they began collecting the caps and playing the milkcap game.

In the 1930s, cap collecting was easy because the Honolulu's Dairymen's Association delivered milk to kids' homes. Kids would collect the caps with printed logos and other designs, asking the milkman for specific cover designs to complete a set.

In the late 1940s to early 1950s the Dairymen's Association pumped up their cap designs: one showed a girl on a swing, others portrayed images from nursery rhymes. When milk sanitation became an issue in the early 1950s, the Dairymen printed messages on a twenty-seven cap series, with information on ways that milk was protected.

are better

It may seem weird, but in parts of the world, milk is still sold in milk bottles, not milk cartons. It's better for our environment to use bottles and the milk tastes way better—not to mention the cool caps you can collect.

The Cap Comeback

A few years ago, the Haleakala Dairy on Maui (one of the Hawaiian Islands) printed special cap designs on their milk bottles as a promotion. At the same time, the dairy launched a new drink called Passion Orange Guava juice. To advertise the drink, they printed "POG" in bright red letters on the milk bottles' caps. Not only did kids start collecting these milkcaps, they started calling the caps and the game they played with them—POG.

In 1991, a Honolulu teacher named Blossom Glabisco was looking for a way to occupy her restless students. Blossom, who was born and raised on Maui, remembered playing a milkcap game. She told her students to save and collect milkcaps and taught them the game. One player stacks five or so milkcaps on the ground and, taking another heavier cap (called a *kini* or a slammer), slams down on the stack. The player keeps whichever caps flip over. Kids loved it and from that time on recess was never the same.

Blossom's niece brought the Haleakala Dairy's POG milkcaps from Maui to Honolulu for Blossom's students. Then kids in Honolulu started calling the milkcap game POG. Pretty soon, hobby stores, card stores, toy stores and grocery stores were selling POGs. By 1993, it was estimated that one billion POGs had circulated the islands of Hawaii.

Visitors from the mainland (what folks in Hawaii call the other forty-nine states) saw POG signs posted in stores, promotional POGs distributed at fast food outlets and kids playing POG—everywhere! One vacationer returned to Newport Beach, California, and told his stockbroker buddy, Bill Hodson, about the Hawaiian POG explosion.

Bill ordered some POGs and decided to design better ones. He also came up with a new name for the caps and game: TROVS as in treasure trove. Armed with TROV samples featuring cartoon Trovinator characters designed by his roommate, Bill flew to Hawaii and got more orders than he thought possible.

In a short time, Bill's TROVS were selling wildly in Hawaii, but he had a bigger dream—to bring TROVS to the mainland. Bill went to neighborhood kids, gave them TROVS, taught them the game and told them to tell all their friends about this cool game. Pretty soon, Bill heard the "thunk" sound of slammers on sidewalks all over his neighborhood.

Bill Hodson

Meanwhile, a retired Southern California businessman, Alan Rypinski, also heard of the milkcap craze sweeping Hawaii. Billions of POGs were passing through kids' hands. "And when I hear the word *billions*," Rypinski says, "I listen." What he heard led him to Maui's Haleakala Dairy where he bought the POG trademark in 1993. Alan came back to the mainland and started the World POG Federation (WPF).

Now the World POG Federation is busy

Leaders
of the Cap

Alan Rypinski

producing authentic POGs (that's how collectors refer to the STANPAC-produced milkcaps), coordinating tournaments nationwide (including the Knott's Berry Farm Southern California POG Championship) and launching a POG character called POGMAN. The WPF's mission is to produce the absolute finest quality milkcaps, and so far they have, making them leaders in the cap industry.

"POG playing is both for boys and girls," says Alan. "And you can be the wimpiest kid and still beat a big, burly football player. Everyone in the family can play. That's the fun of it."

AUTHENTIC MILKCAP PRINTING

Milkcap printing has stayed pretty much the same since the business began. According to **STANPAC**, the leading milkcap manufacturer, it only takes one machine to turn a roll or paperboard into a printed disc. Here's how it happens: A roll of paperboard is fed into the disc-cap

STANPAC, Ontario, Canada

press. Letterpress-style printing heads get ink from an inking roller that comes down to print the paper. The paper then moves through a series of stations:

STATION 1: Creates the pull tab (what you use to pull the milkcap out of the bottle cap). **STATION 2:** Removes the pickout (little cut-out area that allows you to get at the pull tab). **STATION 3:** Inserts a staple from a single spool of wire. **STATION 4:** Cuts out the disc. **STATION 5:** Removes the discs from the web. **STATION 6:** The caps are run through a wax bath and placed in tubes for shipping.

the

game

How to play "the main game" and other variations

Ask any milkcap-playing maniac and he or she will say there's one *main* way to play the game. But that doesn't mean it's the *only* way. Cap players create new games and rules all the time. This chapter covers how to play the "main game" plus some fun variations. Try the variations and even better—come up with you own. Then write and tell us about your game: what it's called and how it's played.

paper

Who's up first?

The first order of business in any game is to figure out who goes first. In cap playing, here are two ways to decide: **Heads or Tails.** A milkcap always has two sides: One is the colorful printed side, the other is blank or has some writing on it. Call the up, colorful side "heads" and the other side "tails." After each of you calls a "heads" or "tails," flip the cap in the air. Whoever picked the side it lands on, goes first.

GETTING STARTED

Rock, Paper, Scissors

In Hawaii, most of the kids use this game (called *Jun Ken Po*) to decide who goes first. The two players face off for three different rounds of rock, paper, scissors. The players secretly decide which of the three signs they will form with their hand. Calling "one, two, three," both players show their hands at the count of three. Remember, paper "covers" (wins over) rock, scissors "cuts" (wins over) paper, rock "smashes" (wins over) scissors.

the main game

Eight Steps To POG Heaven

Usually played with anywhere from two to six players.

1. Each person selects two to three milkcaps from his or her own personal stash. It's better if you play with no more than ten milkcaps total. (So if it's two people playing, each one should put in five caps.)

2. The milkcaps are placed on the game board or any flat surface, white-side-up. (In tournament play, the caps are placed color-side-up.)

3. Flip a cap or do rock, paper, scissors to decide who goes first.

4. The first player takes a slammer (also called a *kini*) and throws it at the stack. There are several ways to toss a slammer. See the slammer section in this chapter.

5. Whatever caps the player flips color-side-up, he or she wins and takes out of play.

6. The remaining caps are then restacked, and the second player tosses a slammer at the stack.

7. The game ends when all the caps have been flipped over, leaving no more in play.

8. The player who is left with the most caps at the end of the game wins.

game variations

Try These Or Make Up Your Own!

BLACK WIDOW

This is the same game as Poison (see opposite page) except there's a black widow spider on the slammer. The player taps around the stack in six different spots and then owns the stack.

CRISS CROSS

In this game, players put a curse on their opponents by taking their slammer and tapping the board or ground above the pile and saying "up," then tapping below the stack and saying "down," then circling the stack with their slammer and saying "all around" and making an X under the pile and saying "criss cross." This curse is supposed to keep their opponent from flipping any caps over.

OUTSIDERS

When someone who is not playing reaches in, grabs the slammer in play out of the air after it bounces off the stack, then the outsider gets to keep the slammer.

POISON

Players first agree on a "dirty game"; then one player pulls out a slammer with the poison symbol (usually a skull and crossbones) on it. The slammer's poison symbol may be in a circle or a triangle. If it's in a circle, the player takes their poison slammer and draws an imaginary circle around the stack of milkcaps. By making this move, the player automatically wins all the stacked caps and the game. If the poison symbol is in a triangle, the player taps three triangle points around the stack and wins the milkcaps. This is called "the power of poison."

Don't even think about...

... hitting the ground after a toss to flip over caps. When that last cap is too hard to flip, a player can add another cap on to the stack.

TORNADO

If the caps fly out of a pile in tornado-like formation, the hitter gets to keep the stack.

BASEBALL

The rules are the same as in baseball. The game is played with four caps in the stack and each player plays through an "inning." Every time a player misses, it's an "out." If the player flips one cap, it's a single run, man on first base. If the player flips two caps, it's a double, men on second and third base. And so on. For example:

1. First player goes, flips over one. This stands for a single hit. The call is one man on base, no outs.

2. Same player goes again and flips over two. Now there is one man on second base, one man on third and no outs.

3. Same player goes again, misses twice. The call is one man on second, one on third and two outs. There's one cap left; if the player turns it over, he or she scores a home run.

4. Same player goes again, misses. That's three outs. Next player is up.

Note: If all four are flipped on the first hit, that would be a home run.

(Game courtesy of The World POG Federation)

YIN YANG

If a player shows a yin yang slammer, this means the player can make up his or her own rules.

COUNTDOWN

Some milkcaps have numbers on the back. If the players are playing for count, the players score the numbers on whatever milkcaps are flipped. The highest score wins.

WAR

The first player lines up four milkcaps in a row on a table and sets the slammer behind them. The second player does the same on the other side of the table. Player number one slides a slammer and tries to knock off the opponent's milkcaps on the other side of the table. Each cap that falls scores a point. The first person to knock all four milkcaps off the table wins.

Rule: Knocking the slammer off does not count for extra points.

EIGHT-BALL

If the game is being played with a milkcap that has the eight-ball on it, the player who flips over the eight-ball automatically gets eight caps from his or her opponent.

(Game courtesy of Upper Stahk)

SKULLS

If the game is being played with a milkcap that has a skull on it, the player who flips over the skull looses his or her slammer and can't collect pieces flipped in that round.

(Game courtesy of Upper Stahk)

"It's the kids' game."

"No authority. No rules. Keep it basic and let kids play their way."
—Bill Hodson, Owner and Founder of TROV

41

SKUNK

If a player does not flip any milkcaps, the player has to put another cap into the stack before player number two takes their turn.

(Game courtesy of Upper Stahk)

FIRE

Balls of fire is not your ordinary milk cap set. Each of the fifteen fire caps has a number on it. That number represents the number of points the cap is worth.

　　1. Each player begins with a set of Balls of Fire and places a minimum of twenty points' worth of caps in the pile. (There is no maximum number of points.) Example: The first player may place two caps on the stack, adding up to twenty points. The second player may decide to put in six caps to total twenty points.

　　2. The players determine who goes first, then take turns slamming and flipping.

　　3. The players add up their points as they go along.

　　4. The first player to reach 100 points, wins!

　　Note: The eight-ball cap is worth double its face value. Only use the eight-ball cap if you have no other choice.

(Game courtesy of JOTS)

SLAMMER SHOOT-OUT

Slammer Shoot Out is basketball for cap players. The 16-inch board has two big hoops in the middle and comes with two different colored slammers, engraved like basketballs. The official game is simple: Players slam their slammers through the hoop for as many points as they agree to award per basket (Players decide on points before "tip-off.") For a little variety, stack caps under the basket to flip. After slamming, count your flipped caps and then take that many more shots. Players are encouraged to make up their own games and can play to as many points as they want.

(Game courtesy of Spontaneous Enterprises, Inc.)

WPF Rules Of The Game

Listen to your teacher.
Respect others.
No playing for keeps.
Be a good sport.
Watch your language.
Be creative.
Learn something new.
Have fun.
Remember, playing POG on campus is
a privilege. Abuse it . . . and lose it.
—World POG Federation

calls
Making the Game More Interesting

X-RAY

When the players are down to the last cap in the stack, the hitter can call "heads or tails" to say which way the cap will land. If the hitter calls it right, he or she wins the cap.

(Courtesy of Melanie Ching's Bottle Cap Map *book)*

GRASSHOPPER

If the player misses the stack but the slammer pops back so that the player can catch it, the player can call "grasshopper" and go again.

REGULAR GAME OR CLEAR RULES

If the player forgets to call "regular rules," the poison slammer can be used to take all milkcaps in the stack. If he or she calls "regular rules," poison doesn't count. The clear game can also be called against grasshopper and "tips" (where the player places their slammer at the edge of the last milkcap to flip it).

NO AFTER CALLS

This means that the players can't call any new rules after the game has begun.

MISS NO COUNT

If the thrower misses the stack, the player has another turn. The amount of misses must be agreed upon.

NO OUT HITTER

Another person can't substitute for a player at any time during the game.

NO SLAPS

The player can't hit the ground or game board to force the cap to turn over.

ANTIDOTE SLAMMER

If a player shows a poison slammer and calls poison, the other player can beat the "poison" by showing an antidote slammer.

(Game courtesy of TROV)

the art of slamming

Hurling, Tossing and Gripping Action

How you tilt your wrist, how fast you toss the slammer, and what kind of aim you have will make all the difference in slamming. Slam champs tell us it's "practice, practice, practice!" Meanwhile, try out some of these fancy slam moves.

OVER STYLE

This move is used most often in tournament play. The player balances the slammer, flat, on the palm side of his or her index and forefinger and turning those two fingers over, releases the slammer onto the stack.

OVER STYLE WITH THUMB

The player lays the slammer on index and forefinger the same way as the "over style," but can use the thumb to grip and help turn the slammer over.

SLICE

The player holds the slammer horizontally between the thumb and index finger (like holding a frisbee) and slices downward onto the milkcap stack. The player can also use this move hitting the stack from the side.

ELEPHANT

Holding the slammer vertically between two fingers, the player flicks the slammer (like a yoyo) downward onto the stack.

SUPRASTRIKER™

Designed by a scientist who helped launch NASA's shuttle mission, the SupraStriker™ is bowl-shaped and is supposed to be a superior hitter.

ROLY-POLY

Holding the slammer upright like a car's tire on the ground, the player rolls the slammer into the stack.

HIGH JUMP

The player aims the slammer high above the stack and drops it.

TIP

Sometimes done with the one remaining milkcap, the player takes the slammer and presses down on the milkcap's side causing it to flip over.

TWISTER

Holding the slammer upright like a car's tire on the ground, the player twirls it into the stack.

slice

two-finger splat

twister

TWO-FINGER SPLAT

Holding the slammer upright like a car's tire on the ground, the player gives the slammer a forefinger flick into the stack.

TWO- OR THREE-FINGERED SLAM

This is the most common slam used in street play. In the two-fingered slam, the player holds the slammer vertically between the thumb and index finger. In the three-fingered slam, the player holds the slammer between the thumb and forefinger with positive pressure supplied by the index finger. The player then lifts and throws the slammer downward onto the stack.

cheat hitter

If you find yourself slammer-less, you can always create a cheat hitter: It's two milkcaps glued or stapled together sometimes with a weight like a quarter or a washer inserted between them.

49

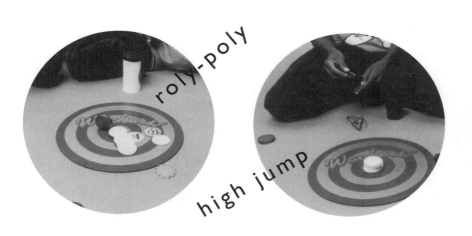

roly-poly

high jump

tipping

Students in Hawaii's Liliuokalani Elementary School 5th and 6th grade class came up with these rules in their

Unofficial Milkcap Handbook:

No stealing.
No selling caps during school hours or on school grounds.
No playing for keeps on school grounds.
No swearing.
You are responsible for your own caps. (Do not ask anyone to watch your caps for you.)
Do not bring valuable caps to school. Bring only enough to play.
No playing caps in class.
Play in an area where you are not blocking the walkway.

tourna

ments

Big groups of kids get together, play caps and win! Yeah!

O nce the milkcap craze hits your neighborhood, it won't be long before tournaments follow. Cap tournaments are held at schools, toy stores, parks, malls and anywhere it's possible to slam and jam. They are usually hosted by the manufacturers and co-hosted by the store, mall or other location where the event is taking place. For instance, the World POG Federation (WPF) hosted one of the largest tournaments at Disneyland in Anaheim, California. Disneyland, of course, acted as the co-host for this WPF tournament.

The WPF call their tournaments "traveling road shows to educate and entertain kids in the art of collecting and playing POG." Most tournaments are guaranteed fun, in fact, at some tournaments, the WPF brings POGMAN (its costumed-fur-ball mascot) and his back-up singers, The Primates, along to perform.

The main purpose of tournaments, though, is for kids to play. Most tournaments charge an entry fee per player. Sometimes the entry fee will mean free caps and a slammer. Other times, it's just a fee to play. At most tournaments, however, no one goes home capless. Tournament play is different from regular play: you play only one on one, use regulation tournament caps and slammers

and have set rules on how to slam and score.

To give you an idea of what it's like, this is how TROV tournaments are run:

The playing area is roped off for "players and judges only."

Playing tables are set up so there are two game sets per table.

Registration begins two hours prior to tournament time. Age groups are set up: six and under, seven to eleven and twelve and up.

Each participant gets a raffle ticket that also is his or her registration number. (At other manufacturer's tournaments, players may get numbers to wear like runners wear in races.)

There are two judges per table; one judge per game set.

tournament rules

The player to go first is decided by a flip of the slammer. The printed side is "heads."

Slammers are held with two fingers, no thumbs. The slam is done in the "over" style. (This means balancing the slammer, flat, on the palm side of your index and forefinger and turning your two fingers over, releasing the slammer onto the stack.)

The first player to flip six caps wins the game. The winner of two out of three games wins the round.

If the player going first flips six on the first try, the opponent is allowed to make one attempt at also flipping all six on a first try. If that player is unsuccessful, pieces are restacked and a new game begins.

Flipped caps must land on the table. Caps off the table do not count.

Any disagreement with a judge's call by a player or parent must be discussed at the time if occurs. The judge has the final say.

The winner of each round advances to the next round.

WPF tournaments are similar but are played with POG brand *kinis* (slammers) and kids play against the clock instead of winning two out of three. The clock keeper times each player for three or five minutes, and whoever wins the most POG during that period, wins the round. Now the WPF has added a new tournament game called Iron Man POG. It goes like this:

The player starts at a white line and runs about 20 feet to a tire.

The player runs around the tire to a barrel where the player's stack is.

The player slams the stack, then runs backward to the next barrel.

The player slams the stack on that barrel before hopping on one foot to the third barrel.

The player slams the stack on the third barrel and then runs to the last barrel.

Before slamming the last stack, the player has to spin five times, slam and then run to the finish line.

Judges give the players two scores in an Iron Man competition: One score is for style, and the other for number of caps flipped. The player with the highest score at the end of the competition wins.

Pro Caps' Huntington Beach Pier Fest Tournament in July 1994 had great prizes, including two GT bikes, a surfboard, two boogie boards, two wet suits, hats and t-shirts. Cowabunga!

pog champ

Eight-year-old Kyle Valley is "a name" in Southern California POG Tournaments. He came in first place at Disneyland's WPF's Championship. We grabbed Kyle for a minute out of his cap-playing day to ask him about life as a POG champ.

Q: How long have you been playing?

A: For about six months. I play mostly with my friends, but I practice with my little sister.

Q: How many caps do you have?

A: I have 400 caps and about 100 *kinis* (slammers). I have three favorite caps: one is a dinosaur that says "I Loved Barney;" one is a yellow face with the tongue sticking out; and the last one has a dune buggy on it.

Q: Do you collect POGs in series?

A: I have almost the whole WPF Series I, the whole Knott's Berry Farm set, the Del Taco set and the Disneyland set with four *kinis*. My dad said to keep them in the pack and don't take them out because they're worth a lot more that way. I keep my individual caps in four shoeboxes in my room.

Q: Do you have a favorite *kini*?

A: It's a metal one with a dinosaur and it's

chomping trees in the forest. Metal *kinis* are the best kind to slam with when you go first or second and there are a lot of caps left in the stack. When there's only one or two caps left, you should use a plastic *kini*.

Q: Is there a cool move with a *kini* you could explain?

A: You lay the *kini* on two fingers and just slam it down really hard on the stack to make the caps flip over.

Q: What's the coolest thing about playing and collecting POGs?

A: It's fun! Everybody has them and they all have really cool designs on them.

At Disneyland's and the World POG Federation's POG Wild tournament in April 1994, 20,000 kids signed up for the California POG Championship scheduled for November of 1994.

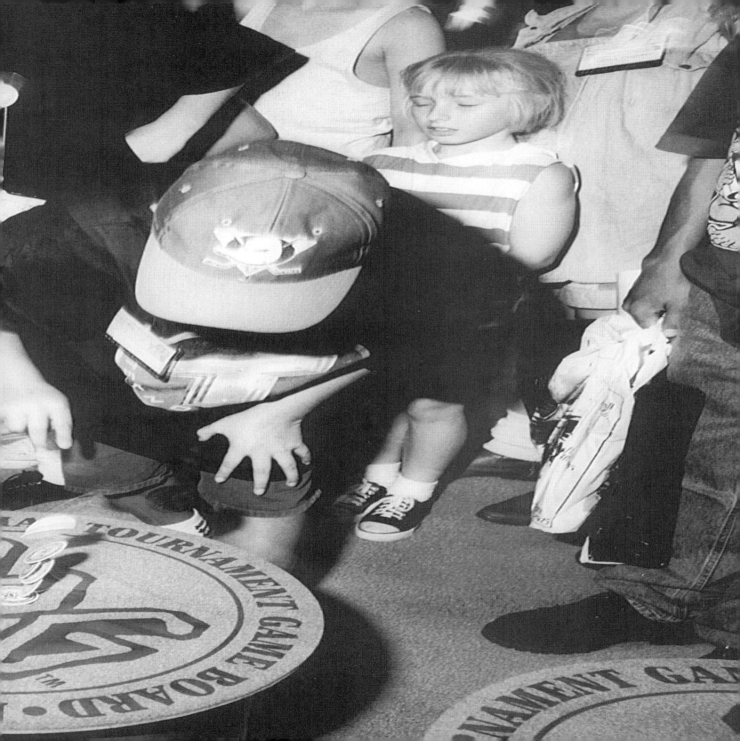

cap

collecting

Which caps to collect, what determines their value and how to preserve your cap collection.

When first kid Chelsea Clinton visited Hawaii with her parents in February of 1993, she was presented with several sets of milkcaps, including a framed set that reportedly hangs in the Oval Office.

Here's some advice for Chelsea: Collect and preserve your caps. They may be valuable one day—if they're not already.

What should you collect and how much are they worth? According to *Collector Caps* magazine, cap value is determined by four things: (1) the **popularity** of the caps (some caps, like Bad Boy and Poison, were immediately popular), (2) the **quality** of the cap (how the cap is printed), (3) the total **quantity** of caps made (some caps are limited editions) and (4) the **availability** of the cap (how easy it is to find).

Here are some tips, offered by cap collectors and manufacturers, to help get you started:

COLLECTING TIP 1

Collect what you like. It's almost impossible to determine which category of caps (sports, cartoon, promotional or other types) will be valuable one day. So the best rule is, if you like it, collect it.

COLLECTING TIP 2

Cap sets, or a series of caps, are a good bet for collecting. For instance, the World POG Federation's (WPF) Wayne Gretzky Coca-Cola Series, Big Apple's The 1969 World Champion Miracle Mets, Rat Cellar Graphix' The Darkness Series I and Collect-A-Card's Mighty Morphin Power Rangers series are good collectibles, if you can find them. If not, collect a new series and preserve it. You never know.

The World POG Federation produced a Wayne Gretzky series with Coca-Cola in Canada. The caps show photos of Gretzky's great performances with play information on the back. The caps were designed for a six week promotion at a Canadian convenience store but were gone within three days. The set of eighteen is valued at $300.

Big Apple Collector, Inc.'s 1969 World Champion Mets 25th Anniversary Commemorative Cap Sheet: In 1969, the Mets overcame hundred-to-one odds and won the World Series. This set includes thirty-one members of the "Miracle Mets" team, featuring the players' team numbers and signatures. Only 25,000 individually numbered sheets complete with a signed certificate of authenticity were released.

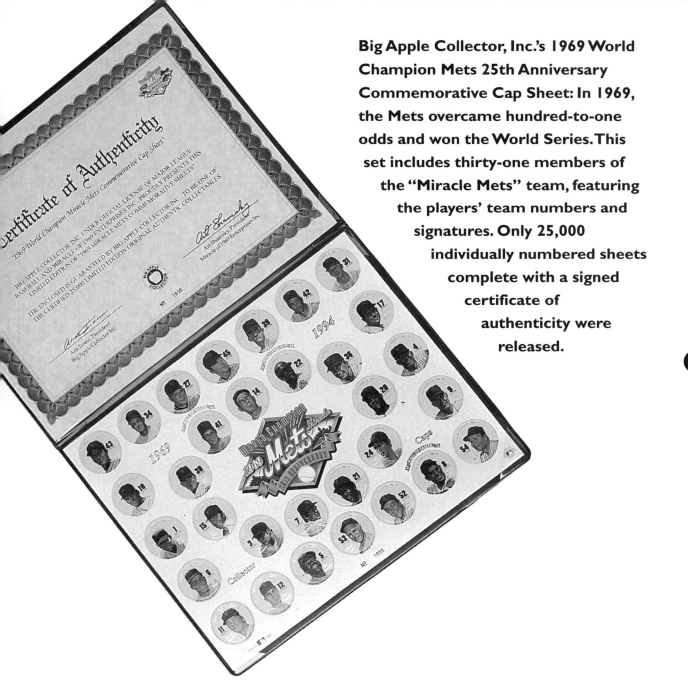

COLLECTING TIP 3

Promotional caps, produced for a special event, are definite collectibles. WPF's Disneyland Spring '94 POG Wild set and the 1994 U.S. Surf Open caps are already worth something today. ⋯⋯⋯⋯⋯⋯⋯⋯⋯⋯⋯⋯⋯▶

COLLECTING TIP 4

Check the art on your caps. Make sure the design is centered evenly on the cap. Also make sure the registration (the clarity of the ink on the drawing) is clear, not fuzzy, faded, smudged or running.

COLLECTING TIP 5

If possible, find out how many of the caps you are interested in collecting were printed. Limited print runs will help boost the cap's value. ⋯⋯⋯⋯⋯⋯⋯⋯⋯⋯⋯⋯⋯⋯⋯⋯⋯▶

COLLECTING TIP 6

Older, original milkcaps from the Dairymen's Association are rare and high-priced. If you are interested in collecting caps, track down experts who know about them. Or you can contact shops in Hawaii that sell original milkcap sets.

COLLECTING TIP 7

Shop around for the best buy. Cap prices may vary, particularly at trading card shows and card and comic shops.

This 1994 edition of the Tournament of Roses milkcap set features Grand Marshall William Shatner and the 1994 Rose Bowl Queen.

Milkcaps are found at coin and hobby shops, toy stores, drugstores, card trading and comic bookstores.

COLLECTING TIP 8

The best time to buy a cap is when it first comes out, especially if you know it's from a limited print run.

COLLECTING TIP 9

If you're into sports caps, you many find better buys on the caps of those sports not in season at the time you're buying. ·····························▶

COLLECTING TIP 10

Unique caps such as 3-D caps, color-changing caps, glow-in-the-dark, hologram caps and solar caps have a good chance of increasing in value. ·····························▶

attention! authentic

From the early 1900s on, the Dairymen Association had about 600 different dairies in Hawaii distributing bottles with caps, but many caps were blank. Cap historians have listed 288 dairies that most likely had a cover or cap imprinted with a designer logo. From the 1930s through 1950s, caps had messages, colors, slogans, even told stories. Many mainland dairies also had cap logos and designs from the early 1900s on. Those are the caps to collect if you're into authentic milkcaps.

the world's most valuable cap

InterIsland Sports Cards produced a 24-karat-gold milkcap series for **TROV** called **TROV** Gold. One side of each cap was minted in 24-karat gold and the other side was marked with a hand-printed serial number. **TROV** put a limited number of these gold caps in their regular sets but also sold them separately for thirty dollars a cap! A **TROV** Gold cap today is said to be worth between fifty to seventy-five dollars each.

cap collectors

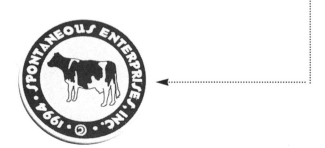

preserving

Now that you've figured out what to collect, here are ways to keep your collection in tip-top shape. Remember, just as with trading cards, value goes down if the caps are bent, soiled or faded, so it's worthwhile to preserve.

PRESERVING TIP 1

Try not to soil your collectible caps. Avoid handling them, but if you need to, make sure your hands are clean. Pick them up by the edge of the cap as you would a CD. Some collectors even wear gloves when handling their collectible caps to prevent discoloration from natural oils or dirt.

PRESERVING TIP 2

Keep the caps covered, away from air and dirt. The best way to do this is by placing the caps in plastic sheets. WPF and other cap companies produce three-ring binders for cap collections. Ultra Pro makes a plastic sheet with a special circle cut to hold fifty-six regular-size caps. Cylindrical plastic containers are also a good way to store caps.

PRESERVING TIP 3

Don't let plastic containing PVC come in contact with your milk caps. PVC bleeds over time and will stain your caps.

PRESERVING TIP 4

Store your caps in a cool, dry location.

Some kids carry POGs in Ziplock bags, while some carry them in colorful cylinders decorated with cartoon characters or logos.

most wanted

According to the latest issues of *Collector Cap* magazine, these are top collecting choices based on quality, manufacturing process, theme, licensing, availability and number of caps produced:

Slammers by SlamCo

Power Caps by Collect-A-Cap

Knott's Berry Farm Collectors Set Series 1 by WPF

Wyland set of 20

15 Balls of Fire by JOTS

Poison Caps

Disneyland POGWild Set by WPF

California State Qualifier by WPF

Street Fighter II

Flintstones by Pacific Rim Trading Caps

Yin Yang

Madonna Muzic Pogz

1969 World Champion Miracle Mets

World POG Federation

Hi-C Marvel X-Men

Sabritas

A WPF Disneyland *kini* **is valued at $25. A WPF Disneyland POG is valued at $10.**

collector's hit list

Bob Young's column in the *Honolulu Observer* suggests collectors watch for these caps:

STANPAC's first promotional caps, including Hawaiian Air, 7-Eleven and McDonalds sets

Haleakala Dairy's POG

Wailua Elementary School's Bulldog caps (This is the school where Blossom Glabisco teaches and where Hawaii's recent POG craze started.)

Honolulu Police Department's D.A.R.E. caps (This caps series came out soon after Blossom's students rediscovered milkcaps. The Honolulu Police Department was the first to recognize the value of putting anti-drug messages on milkcaps.)

Moorpark, California's, sheriff's unit uses these D.A.R.E. caps to reward kids who do things right: like wearing bicycle helmets or crossing streets safely.

SkyCap series:

Famous trading card maker, SkyBox, produced the Superman SkyCap Series as their first release. (It contained the four fake DC Comics Supermen and a slammer.) The second series was called DC SkyCaps and included fifty-four caps of top Super Heroes and Super Villains. The third was the Batman Knightfall line, and the fourth, a series of *Jurassic Park* SkyCaps. The last series SkyCap produced was the Jim Lee SkyCaps, a seventy-two-cap set, featuring characters from Jim Lee's comics such as WildC.A.T.S., Storm Watch and DeathBlow.

The WPF includes this supercool checklist with some of their cap sets. It's a handy way to figure out which caps you have and which ones you need.

slammers and game boards

Hawaiians say mainlanders have taken slammers to new heights. And they're right. The newest slammers range in thickness and are made with all sorts of materials: wood, pewter, chrome, acrylic and even iron. Shredder slammers have jagged edges (not recommended for safe play). And the "metal monsters" tend to bend milkcaps and damage game boards. But slammers, like caps, are collectible. A tip for slammer collectors: thick, paper slammers were the originals and therefore have more value.

Game boards are on the popularity fast track because more and more cap manufacturers are producing the colorful boards made of wood, cork, cloth or plastic. Game-board sizes range from coaster size to Frisbee size and may have value one day.

MOON CASTER

pog wild

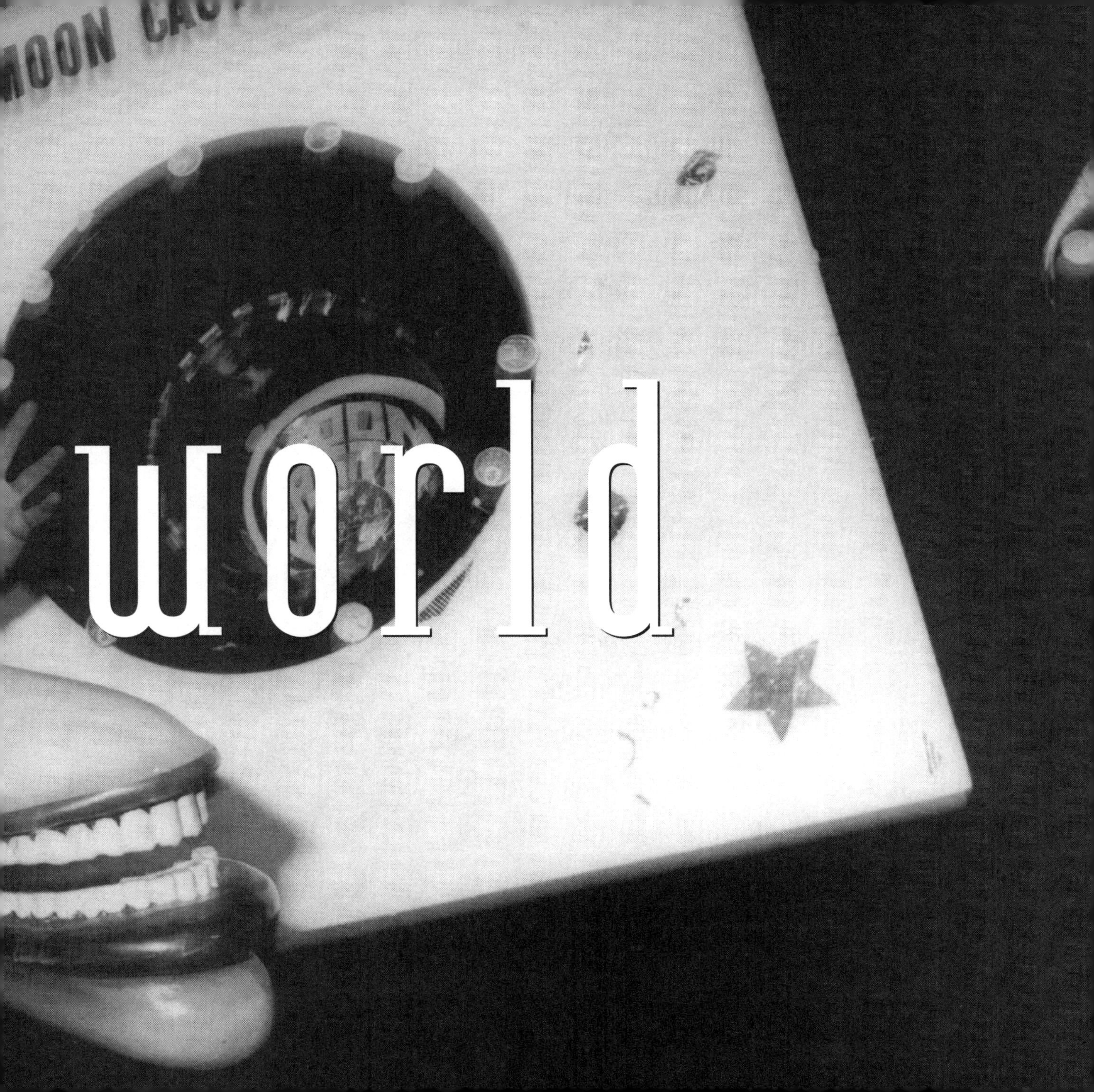

world

Clubs, newsletters, cap characters and much more!

Not everything in POG world is round and flat. There is a POGMAN, a TROVinator, videos, and even design-your-own milkcaps. Here are some fun things we found in POG world:

POGMAN

He's the World POG Federation's most lovable rascal. This matted ball of fur appears on authentic POG milkcaps and displays. Don't be surprised if you run into POGMAN at your local mall and watch out: he's got a major attitude!

POG-TOGRAPHY

Thanks to the World POG Federation, everyone can have a personalized POG. Yep, a photograph of *you* can appear on a POG or *kini* (as the WPF likes to call slammers). The POG-TOGRAPHY system is a one-of-a-kind, portable video imaging system. Contact the World POG Federation to find out where a POG-TOGRAPHY system is set up near you or if you can send away for your personalized POG.

THE TROVINATOR

The TROVinator is a comic book character with multiple personalities; he turns into TROVmaster, TROVslayer, and even a female TROVina. The character was created for TROV and his mission is to guide a young boy, Trevor Trov, through different adventures.

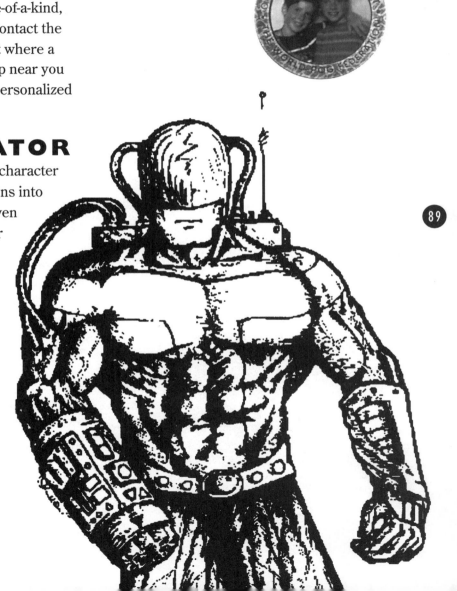

89

CAP-A-DOODLE

Think you can create better images than the ones on caps out there? Now's your chance with the Cap-A-Doodle kit: it has eight blank caps, three color markers and mylar finishing seals. The caps you create will certainly be one-of-a-kind. And who knows, maybe even a collector item.

SPI KAPS™ DESIGN YOUR OWN HITTER

The SPI KAPs designer hitter kits come with an assortment of stickers and two blank acrylic slammers, so guess what? You can decorate your slammers your way! Place a sticker off-center or pile all the stickers on one slammer. You are the master of your slammer.

MOONCASTER

The object is to place your cardboard caps in this boomerang-shaped disc launcher called a Mooncaster. With a flick of the wrist, your caps can fly up to 200 feet! The Mooncaster's creator came up with the game when he discovered that the cardboard milkcaps can really fly.

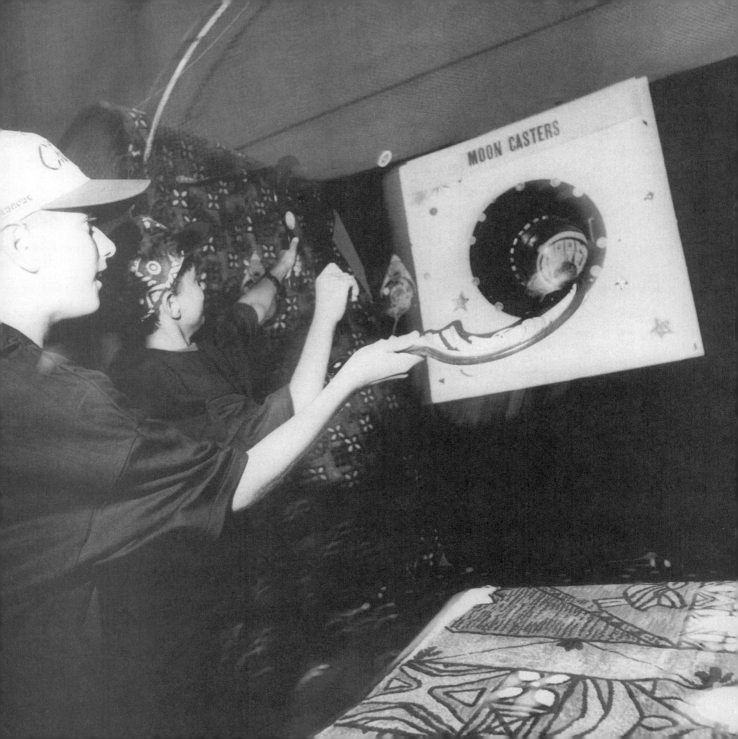

TK KAPS

These caps can be traded in for t-shirts, hats, water bottles, a TK game board, slammers, and other merchandise. Just send in the number of TK's required for the item of your choice. No money, no proof of purchase or verification required. Just send in authentic TKs you have traded.

For more information on where to buy TK Kaps, call or write:

TK™ KAPS Inc.
10153 Riverside Drive #600
North Hollywood, CA 91603
800/TK2-POGS

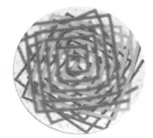

Cap Stuff to Read and Watch

Joining a cap club or just reading a regular newsletter will keep you up to speed on the latest happenings in milkcap land. Here are some companies who produce newsletters, have clubs, and even a couple of videos to check out:

NEWSLETTERS

American Game Caps

A monthly newsletter sent to cap lovers on the mailing list. Want to be on the list? Contact:

410 W. Fletcher
Orange, CA 92665
(714) 921-2277
FAX: (714) 921-4827

JM Productions

From the maker of the Juan Pollo milkcap series comes "Cap & Slam Action," a tabloid for kids.

For more information, write:
PO Box 2081
Sun City, CA 92586-2081
909/672-4455

JOTS WORLD

A quarterly newsletter with information on tournaments, new JOTS and more. To get on the mailing list, write to:

JOTS™
1609 E. McFadden Ave. Suite F
Santa Ana, CA 92705

TROV Talk

A monthly newsletter for TROVinators. You can also send the name of a friend or relative who doesn't live in California or Hawaii and TROV will send them a slammer with your compliments! To get on the mailing list and to refer a friend or relative, write to:

TROV®USA
189 Business Center Drive
Corona, CA 91720
Or call:
(800) 862-TROV

VIDEOS

Milkcap Mania: Volumes 1 and 2

Volume one is about playing caps and slammers, volume two is about collecting caps and slammers. You can find these videos wherever videos are sold. If you can't find them write to:

 3-G Home Video
 8025 Deering Ave.
 Canoga Park, CA 91304
 or call: (800) 345-5855

The Legend of the Hawaiian Slammers

Produced by DIC Entertainment and distributed by Buena Vista Home Video, this action-adventure animated show will also be aired on TV.

Searching for POG: The Video

Herbie J. Winkleman, rookie newspaper reporter, goes searching for POG in this wacky adventure video produced by the World POG Federation. Sold wherever videos are sold or write to:

 World POG Federation™
 P.O. Box 1998
 Newport Beach, CA 92659

MAGAZINES/ GUIDES

Collector Caps Price Guide

The complete guide for milkcap collectors.
For a subscription, write to:

P.O. Box 25753
Honolulu, Hawaii 96825

The Bottle Cap Map

Volumes one and two are available of this
collector's guide to milk bottle covers by
Melanie Ching. Write to:

2961 D Kalawao Place
Honolulu, Hawaii 96822
Or call: (808) 988-4547

BOOKS

Coverama

Cap historian DeSoto Brown chronicles the
birth of milkcaps in Hawaii from the earliest
days in the 1920s through the 1950s. The
book is available by mail order. For
information, write to:

Pacific Monograph
1124 Kahili Street
Kailua, Hawaii 96734

MORE CAP INFO

Be a TROV Captain

Send a postcard with your name, age,
address, sex, name of school, grade, and a
sentence on why you should be the Trouncin'
TROV Captain for your area to:

TROV™USA
189 Business Center Drive
Corona, CA 91720
Or call: (800) 862-TROV

World POG Federation

Kids can become official members of the
World POG Federation. Applicants will
receive a membership kit and a one year
subscription to a World POG Federation
newsletter.

For more information, write to:
World POG Federation
P.O. Box 1998
Newport Beach, CA 92659

milkcap

hunting

HEAVY METAL
POISON
TUBE
SLAMMER
HEAVY METAL
10
CAPS
$4.00
BEWARE
$1.00
POISON TUBE
24 TUBES PER BOX

Where to buy caps, how to get free ones, and who makes 'em.

The biggest question about collecting caps is where to get them.

If you're interested in owning caps, the first places to check are your local card and comic-book stores and toy stores. To find the nearest one, look in the phone book under "Baseball Cards" or "Comic Books," or "Toy Stores." Many shops have trays full of hundreds of different caps and slammers.

Caps cost anywhere from five cents to as much as $3 each. Slammers usually start at fifty cents. Some manufacturers "bundle" milkcaps by putting fifty caps in a bag and selling the bag for $5.

DISNEY'S Snow White

SNOW WHITE

SAN DIEGO WILD ANIMAL PARK

1st Edition © Kellarney

Promotional Caps

You don't have to have lots of money to start your milkcap collection. There are tons of places that you can get them for FREE! Businesses give away milkcaps to promote an event, or a product, and it's a great chance for you to rake in some really cool caps.

Whether it's a POG tournament or your local supermarket, there are mondo milkcaps available for the asking. You may have to buy a little something to get it, but the fact that these promotional caps are usually limited editions make them worth the price of a soda or hamburger—especially if you were going to buy one anyway! Here are some of the most popular promotional caps:

DISNEYLAND'S

"Go POG Wild and Rollerblade Crazy" event turned the park into a POG Play Zone during Spring Break '94. At the event, sponsored by the World POG Federation and Rollerblade, kids received free limited edition caps and kinis, which now are valued at $10 to $25.

KNOTT'S BERRY FARM

sponsored the Southern California POG Championship in September 1994. The World POG Federation set up a POG Tournament Play Zone for the whole month of August, leading up to the championships. Kids who participated received a POG ticket, redeemable for a limited edition set of Knott's Berry Farm milkcaps.

DEL TACO'S

220 restaurants in Southern California gave away a Del Taco POG with every Coca-Cola product purchased during August 1994. The limited edition set of twenty POG milkcaps featured World POG Federation characters, Coke and Del Taco designs, as well as the logo for Anaheim's Mighty Ducks.

COCA-COLA CANADA,

in cooperation with the World POG Federation and hockey superstar Wayne Gretzky, manufactured a POG brand milkcap set of eighteen milkcaps which were given away with bottles of Coke purchased at Mac's convenience stores in Canada. The promotion was designed to last six weeks; the caps were gone in three days! The complete set of eighteen is now valued at $300.

SAN DIEGO WILD ANIMAL PARK

designed a series of three milkcaps to give away to kids at the gate during Summer 1994. They currently are working on a larger series to distribute that features photos from the San Diego Zoo's opening in 1911.

At the U.S. OPEN OF SURFING,

held in Huntington Beach ("Surf City"), California, from August 2 to 7 1994, limited edition caps with the event logo were available for fans. *Surfing Magazine* also distributed its own cap at the event.

DRUG ABUSE RESISTANCE EDUCATION (D.A.R.E)

departments in California have designed caps to give to kids involved in the program and those in the community caught in the act—of doing something good! Some of the caps feature the "care bear" of the D.A.R.E. program, local D.A.R.E. logos, McGruff the Crime Dog and county sheriff badges.

FOX TELEVISION NETWORK

has planned a cap series coinciding with the debut of "The Tick," a new animated series airing on the FOX Kids Network this fall.

FAST-FOOD RESTAURANTS

like McDonald's, Carl's Jr. and Burger King, have printed milkcaps with their logos and characters that come with kids' meals or can be purchased for around twenty-five cents extra with a regular menu item.

KING HAWAIIAN BAKERY & RESTAURANT

produced a set of three Chameleon color-changing milkcaps. You can purchase the set for $4.50 or get one of the series for twenty-five cents when you order a kid's meal off the King's *keiki* menu. The King's Hawaiian Bakery set is only available at the Torrance, California, bakery.

CRAIG 'N CO.

produced by JOTS™ features Craig Taubman and his Craig 'n Company rock and roll band. Craig 'n Company's concerts are usually festive including preshow "not ready for bedtime" stories, pajama fashion shows, and the milkcap giveaways.

THE CAP 'N COVER™

produces collectible, limited edition bonditterboppers™ (caps). THE SAFE NEIGHBORHOOD SERIES™ has inspirational messages to help create better, safer communities and comes with a certificate of authenticity.

JUAN POLLO

(pronounced Wan Po Yo), a chain of Southern California chicken restaurants, are selling a cap series called Juan Pollo's Crazy Cousins™. The set also includes a slammer called "The Chicken Lickin' Slammer."

JOTS' Craig 'n Co.

DAIRY QUEEN

BONDITTERBOPPER

JUAN POLLO

DIVE RESTAURANT, Los Angeles

SAN DIEGO WILD ANIMAL PARK

BURGER KING KIDS CLUB

U. S. OPEN OF SURFING

KING'S HAWAIIAN BAKERY

SEA WORLD

Chameleon Caps change color and show hidden designs by placing the cap between your palms and rubbing them together. Chameleon also designs a color-changing Shamu cap for Sea World.

manufacturers

For more information about milkcaps or where to find a certain brand, you can contact the manufacturer. Here is a partial list of current cap manufacturers. Keep in mind there are new brands popping up every day—some even have special newsletters or videos to keep you informed of the latest cap crazes!

American Game Caps™
410 W. Fletcher
Orange, CA 92665
(714) 921-2277
FAX: (714) 921-4827

Big Apple Collector Pogs
714 Atlantic Avenue
Baldwin, NY 11510
(800) 650-5414

The California Milk Cap Co.
909 N. Lidford Ave.
La Puente, CA 91744
(818) 968-6962
FAX: (818) 968-5363

The Cap 'n Cover™
300 Carlsbad Village Drive
Suite 108 A-199
Carlsbad, CA 92008
(619) 434-9573
FAX: (619) 434-9935

Chameleon™
4328 S. Victoria Avenue
Los Angeles, CA 90008
(213) 291-1752
FAX: (213) 291-7708

Collect-A-Card
P.O. Box 17588
Greenville, SC 29606-8588
(800) 675-5950
FAX: (803) 675-5950

Collegiate Caps™
11702 Via El Mercado
Los Alamitos, CA 90720
(310) 598-8157
FAX: (310) 594-8880

Custom Caps™
770 Kapiolani Blvd.
Suite 604
Honolulu, Hawaii 96813
(800) CAPS-636
in Hawaii (808) 533-0324

Jam Caps
210 N. Smith Ave.
Corona, CA 91720
(909) 734-8486

JOTS™ USA, Inc.
1609 E. McFadden Ave.
Suite F
Santa Ana, CA 92705
(714) 953-3065
(714) 972-8021
FAX: (714) 973-6304

KEI Collector Caps
20546 Covina Hills Road
Covina, CA 91724
(714) 751-0217

King of POG
2415 Jerusalem Ave.
Suite 106
Bellmore, NY 11710
(516) 781-2626
FAX: (516) 781-2685

Laserform®
22359 Meekland Ave.
Hayward, CA 94541
(510) 537-5267
(800) 523-1081
FAX: (510) 537/9360

Pacific Rim Trading Cards™
P.O. Box 1399
Newport Beach, CA 92663
(714) 722-1766
FAX: (714) 722-7049

SkyBox International
300 North Duke Street
P.O. Box 30009
Durham, NC 27702-3009
(919) 933-4327
•Suggests kids visit their local comics stores for more information about caps.

SlamCo
2752 Woodlawn Drive
Suite 5-109
Honolulu, Hawaii 96822
(808) 988-5180
FAX: (808) 988-5489

Spi Kap™
SafeCo Plastics Inc.
7192 Patterson Drive
Garden Grove, CA 92641
(714) 893-5000
FAX: (714) 892-9017

Spontaneous Enterprises, Inc.
1570 E. Edinger, Unit I
Santa Ana, CA 92705
(714) 835-8482

TK™ KAPS Inc.
10153 Riverside Drive #600
North Hollywood, CA 91603
(818) 566-3666
(800) TK2-POGS

TROV®USA
189 Business Center Drive
Corona, CA 91720
(800) 862-TROV

Universal POGS©
Legends II, Inc.
15801 Graham Street
Huntington Beach, CA 92649
(714) 891-0054
FAX: (714) 894-8380

Upper Deck
5909 Sea Otter Place
Carlsbad, CA 92008-6621
(619) 929-6559

Upper Stahk, Inc.™
2814 N. batvia Ave.
Orange, CA 92665
(714) 282-2255

Wackers™
by On The Ball
P.O. Box 90663
Pasadena, CA
(818) 449-5860

World POG™ Federation
PO Box 1998
Newport Beach, CA 92659
(714) 548-2600
FAX: (714) 548-3377

Z Comic Caps
27075 Cabot Road
Suite 112
Laguna Hills, CA 92653
(714) 582-5076
FAX: (714) 582-5076

103

cap

speak

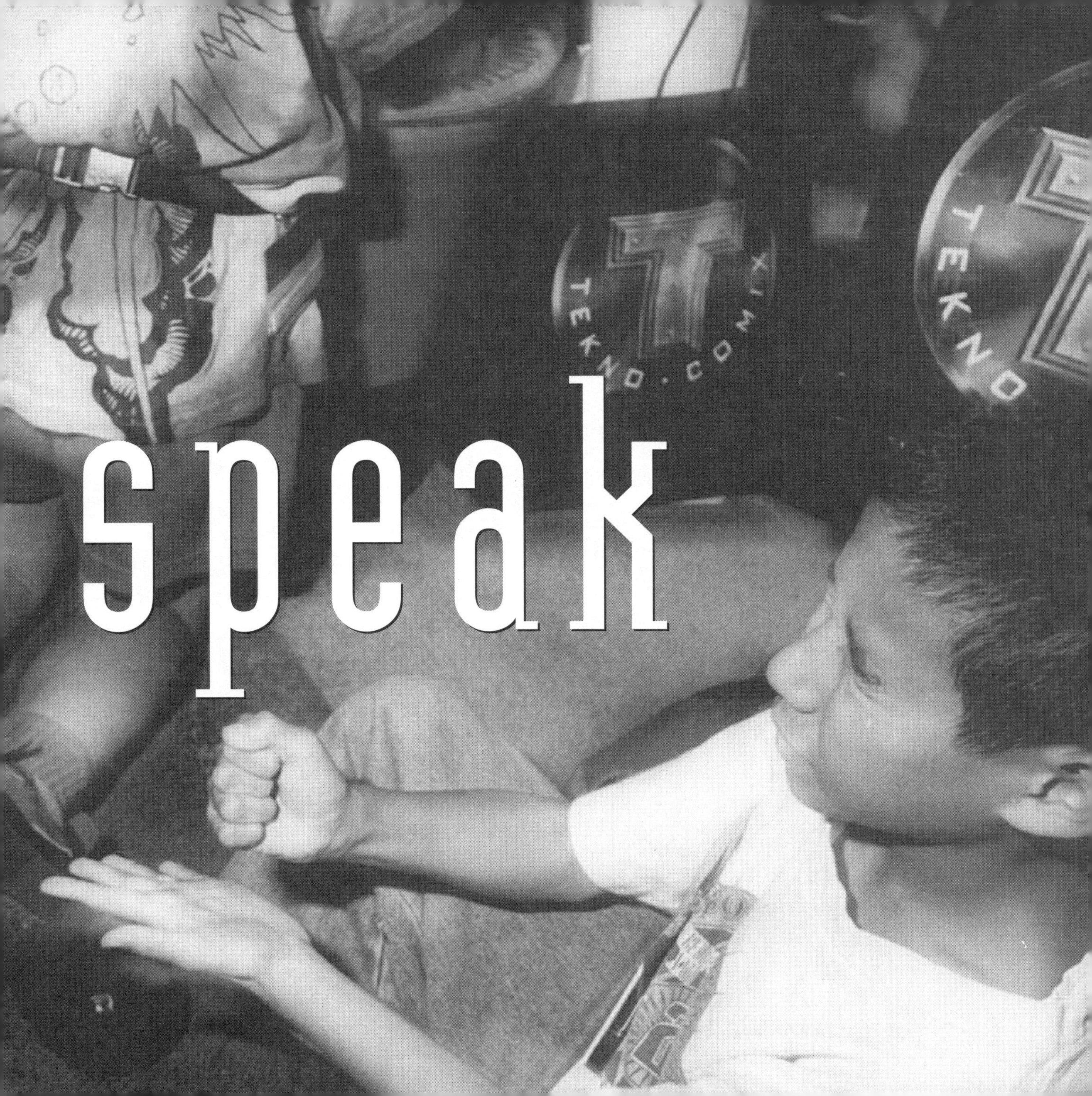

Sure, you can slam, blast, flip and slice a stack. But how's your POG Talk? Check out everything your mouth needs to know for playing and saying POG.

Ante Up: an equal amount of caps to put in stack agreed on by players.

Arena: brightly designed trays on which the milkcap game is played.

Big Daddy: two slammers glued together to slam down harder and flip over more caps.

Blaster: a heavy plastic or metal disc that is thrown down to flip milkcaps over. Also known as a hitter, *kini,* pounder or slammer.

Bracing: padding the last milkcap, by placing something underneath it, because it's the hardest to flip.

Bridging: A player can slant the stack of caps at an angle so it's easier to flip them.

Cap: (also known as milkcap or disc) a silver-dollar-size, cardboard or plastic circle similar to the ones used to seal old-fashioned milk bottles. Decorated with colorful designs, cartoon characters, sports figures, surfing and team logos, comic book heroes, dinosaurs, stamped foil or other designs to give them a slick, glossy look. Brands/other names include: JOTS, HeroCaps, POGs, Power Caps, SkyCaps, TROVs and Tonx.

Cheat Hitters: a homemade slammer made by gluing or stapling two milkcaps together with a weight, like a quarter or washer, stuck between them.

"Check the Back, Jack": World POG Federation slogan; tells kids to check the back of their caps for World POG Federation wallpaper and cap numbers to see if it's an authentic POG.

Coffer: cylindrical plastic containers used to hold milkcaps.

Coffin: plastic TROV container shaped like a coffin: lid opens like a coffin and TROVS stack sideways in container.

Dirty Game: game played with no rules; both players must agree to play a dirty game.

Disc: see cap description.

Double Flips: If the cap flips twice, the person who slammed gets to go again.

Elephant Slam: a method of slamming; player takes the slammer between two fingers and flicks his or her wrist down, releasing the slammer onto the stack.

Faux Caps: cardboard pieces without STANPAC's functional pull tab, staple (used to hold the tab in place) and paraffin coating.

Hitter:
1. a heavy, plastic or metal disc that is thrown down to flip milkcaps over. Also known as a blaster, hitter, *kini* or slammer. 2. the player who is slamming.

Jun Ken Po:
Hawaiian for "Rock, paper, scissors." Method of determining who will go first in a game.

Kini:
a heavy, plastic or metal disc that is thrown down to flip milkcaps over. Also known as a blaster, hitter, pounder or slammer.

Licked:
disqualified; a player is "licked" when he or she licks their slammer in order to make more milkcaps flip over.

Milkcap:
see cap description.

No After Calls:
rule stating players can't create new rules after the game has begun.

Official Slamming Kini:
plastic kini distributed and used by the World POG Federation in official World POG Federation Tournaments.

POG:
1. street game where players attempt to flip over a stack of milkcaps by "slamming" a heavier cap down on top of it; similar to marbles. 2. a brand of milkcaps. 3. an acronym for Passion, Orange, Guava.

Poglodyte:
surfboard riding, furry animal shown on original POG milkcaps.

Pounder:
a heavy, plastic or metal disc that is thrown down to flip milkcaps over. Also known as a hitter, *kini* or slammer.

Shredder:
slammer with ridges.

Slam Boards:
a raised, plastic pad that comes in a variety of designs; preserves your milkcaps from nicks and scratches. Also known as a trouncer pad.

Slammer:
a heavy, plastic or metal disc that is thrown down to flip milkcaps over. Also known as a blaster, *kini* or pounder.

Slice:
a method of slamming; player takes the slammer and slams it down on the stack sideways. Also known as a Sideswipe.

Stacked:
a player who flips over all their milkcaps.

STANPAC:
a Canadian company that produces authentic milkcaps with pull tabs, staples and paraffin coating.

Trouncer Bouncer:
mini Ping-Pong paddle recessed area in middle of a slam board; used as a tool to slam more caps.

index

ADDITIONAL PHOTO CREDITS
Bill Hodson, page 26, courtesy of TROV
Alan Rypinski, page 27, courtesy of World POG Federation
Slammer Shoot-Out, page 42, all photos, page 90, Hawaiian Slammers, page 94, all by Chris Fithian
POGMAN, pages 43, 88, courtesy of World POG Federation
POG Champ, page 62, courtesy of Mrs. Valley
TROVinator, page 89, courtesy of TROV